D0465042

EARTH APPLES

Also by Edward Abbey

FICTION

Jonathan Troy
The Brave Cowboy
Fire on the Mountain
Black Sun
The Monkey Wrench Gang
Good News
The Fool's Progress
Hayduke Lives!

NONFICTION

Desert Solitaire
Slickrock
Cactus Country
The Hidden Canyon
Appalachian Wilderness
The Journey Home
Abbey's Road
Desert Images
Down the River
Beyond the Wall
*Slumgullion Stew (The Best
    of Edward Abbey)*
One Life at a Time, Please
*A Voice Crying in the
    Wilderness*
*Confessions of a Barbarian:
    Selections from the
    Journals of Edward
    Abbey*

EARTH APPLES

(Pommes de Terre)

THE POETRY OF EDWARD ABBEY

Collected and Introduced by David Petersen
Original Artwork by Michael McCurdy

ST. MARTIN'S PRESS / NEW YORK

EARTH APPLES. Copyright © 1994 by Clarke C. Abbey. Illustrations copyright © 1994 by Michael McCurdy. All rights reserved. Printed in the United States of America. No part of this book may be used or reproduced in any manner whatsoever without written permission except in the case of brief quotations embodied in critical articles or reviews. For information, address St. Martin's Press, 175 Fifth Avenue, New York, N.Y. 10010.

Design by Jaye Zimet

ISBN 0-312-11265-3

First Edition: September 1994

10 9 8 7 6 5 4 3 2 1

Contents

Introduction   xi

Confessions: 1951–1965

The Whole Fucking Crew   *3*
November, 1951—Edinburgh   *4*
December, 1951—Edinburgh   *5*
December, 1951—Edinburgh II   *6*
February, 1952—Edinburgh   *8*
Verse Provoked by a Recent Visit to the Stacks   *9*
January, 1952—Majorca   *10*
January, 1952—Majorca II   *11*
March, 1952—Edinburgh   *12*
April, 1952—on the North Sea   *13*
April, 1952—on the North Sea II   *14*
Brief Speech to a Weather Vane   *15*
April, 1952—on the North Sea III   *16*
May, 1952—Norway   *17*
May, 1952—Norway II   *18*
Feudalism   *19*
Terror and Desire   *20*
The Wild Dove   *22*
Flash Flood   *23*
August, 1956—Arches   *25*

August, 1956—Arches II   *26*
August, 1959—Albuquerque   *28*
The Writer   *29*
Ditty   *30*
July, 1965—Arches   *31*
Episodes and Visions   *32*
A Few Appropriate Lines from Burns   *33*
A Maxim   *34*

POEMS AND SHARDS: 1965–1970

Book I: Poems for Judy

Love Letter   *39*
The Gift   *40*
Love Poem   *42*
Song from the City   *43*
Soaring Song   *44*
North Rim   *46*
Idle Music   *47*

Book II: Occasions

A Simple-Minded Song of Hatred   *51*
One Thing at a Time, for Christ's Sake   *54*
Manhattan at Twilight, Seen from the
    Palisades   *56*

Book III: Notes & Illuminations from a Burning Book

King Aethelstan to All Heads . . .   *59*

Pommes de Terre   *60*

A Dream   *61*

Last Rites   *62*

Peace & Plenty   *63*

From a Sundown Legend   *64*

Where Is Your Rock?   *65*

Due Notice   *66*

What Zapata Said   *67*

Inconsolable Memories   *68*

Essay on Time   *69*

Long Poem: A Few Words for Some of
    My Contemporaries   *71*

For the Old Man   *76*

On the Birth of My Son   *78*

Book IV: Love's Bawdy

Frivolous Question   *81*

Two Profane Love Songs   *82*

I Wish   *84*

I Don't Want Them All (I Just Want All the
    Ones I Want)   *85*

Mornings in Santa Fe, Dead in Death Valley   *86*

Book V: Desert Music

Black Sun   *89*

Down the River   *90*

The Dry Season   *92*

Ambition   *94*

American Picnic   *96*

An Evening Star   *97*

Desert Music   *98*

A Sonnet for Everett Ruess   *101*

CONFESSIONS: 1972–1989

Last Thoughts While Lost Below Lizard
Rock   *105*

Three Limericks   *106*

For Marcel Proust, et al.   *107*

For Clarke   *108*

The Kowboy and His Kow   *109*

Benedictio   *110*

About the Author   *111*

About the Editor   *112*

Herman has taken to writing poetry. You need not tell
anyone, for you know how such things get around.

—in a letter from Mrs. Melville to her mother, 1859,
as quoted in *Confessions of a Barbarian: Selections
from the Journals of Edward Abbey*

INTRODUCTION

*I don't see how poetry can ever be easy. . . . Real poetry,
the thick dense intense complicated stuff that lives and
endures, requires blood and sweat; blood and sweat are
essential elements in poetry as well as behind it.*

—Edward Abbey

My late friend Edward Abbey preferred to think of
himself as a novelist, and in fact published eight fictional
works, including the immortal *The Brave Cowboy*, the
anarchic *The Monkey Wrench Gang*, and his semiauto-
biographical "fat masterpiece," *The Fool's Progress*. Of
the eight, seven remain in print (all but his first, *Jonathan
Troy*, written when he was but twenty-five) and continue
to sell like proverbial hotcakes. Two of Abbey's novels,
The Brave Cowboy and *Fire on the Mountain*, have
been filmed and a third, *The Monkey Wrench Gang*,
is presently under option to Hollywood.

Not bad for a spud-digging farm boy out of rural
Pennsylvania.

But, to paraphrase Ed's good friend Doug "Hay-
duke" Peacock, Abbey's opinion of his own work is only
one among many, and Ed will likely be remembered as
much for his fourteen volumes of literary nonfiction as for

his novels. And few, except perhaps the author himself, would dispute the proposal that the high point in Abbey's literary career was his prose masterpiece, *Desert Solitaire*.

But . . . Cactus Ed as *poet*? Where does poetry fit in the big picture of Abbey's literary accomplishments?

Well, it doesn't, really. This collection, in fact, is something of an anomaly, not proffered as great poetry, but rather, offered as a revealing and entertaining insight into the mind and emotions of a great contemporary novelist and essayist, a great man. For Ed, writing poetry was alternately cathartic and playful, but never, it seems, intended to be "the thick dense intense complicated stuff . . . [requiring] blood and sweat" on the poet's part. Yet, because the seventy-one works contained in these pages are absolutely and irrefutably *Edward Abbey*, they are sure to "live and endure."

Abbey's immutable iconoclasm and nonconformity—which he preferred to think of as "anarchy"—the alternating joy and pain that marked his life, as well as the unique and eloquent voice used to express it, shine through in this collection, the only collection of Abbey's poetry that has ever been or ever will be.

Although he rarely published his poetry, and only occasionally read it in public, Ed nonetheless was a passionate producer of verse. Most often, he drafted a poem in a single go, writing in longhand in his journals and rarely revising. All but a few of the selections contained herein come undiluted from the twenty-one volumes of journal notebooks Abbey kept across the last thirty-eight years of his eventful life. And all were written between November, 1951—when Abbey was twenty-four and a Fulbright fellow studying literature and philosophy at Edinburgh University, Scotland—and March, 1989, when he died at age sixty-two.

The early journals contain Abbey's original poems mixed in freely with the works of others, many of the latter quite obscure and copied into the journals without attribution or quotation marks. Consequently, my most daunting chore in the editing of this collection has been to cull these non-Abbey works from the true *pommes*. After asking several well-read others to go over the collection, and after consulting poetry indexes for titles, first lines, and key words, I do believe the collection offered here is pure Abbey. But there are literally millions of poems in print, I haven't read them all, and I could be wrong. You'll let me know about that, I'm sure.

Earth Apples comprises three sections. The opening (1951 to 1966) and closing (1972 to 1989) *Confessions* sections together contain thirty-four raw "apples" harvested directly from the journals . . . with two exceptions, duly noted, both of which were written during the mid-1950s Arches years and appeared in *Desert Solitaire.*

Sandwiched between these two sections are another thirty-seven pieces that Ed had lifted from his journals during the 1970s, polished, and sorted into five "Books," apparently thinking to publish the lot under the title *Poems & Shards: 1965–1970.* He never got around to it.

Earth Apples derives from the French equivalent, *Pommes de Terre,* and is the author's idea, indirectly at least, dating back to 1951. Although the common French phrase translates literally as "apples of the earth," or "earth apples," it is generally understood, and used, to mean "potatoes." In his early journals, Abbey often employed the personal slang term "pomes" (rhymes with gnomes) as a comically self-disparaging reference to his own poetic efforts, which, it seems, he never took too seriously. After visiting France in late 1951, he added the second *m,* converting "pomes" to *pommes,* apparently pleased to think of his earthy poesy as "spuds." Some years later, he penned a nostalgic open-verse celebration of his childhood recollection of the harvest of a bumper potato crop, calling it "*Pommes de Terre.*"

Thus, *Earth Apples* seemed predestined to serve as the title of this tasty little volume.

Concerning the titles of individual poems: All of the center-section "Book" pieces wear the names given them by the author in his journals. When known, I have added date and location of writing in parentheses.

But many of the works in the opening and closing *Confessions* sections appear in the journals untitled. Consequently, rather than employ the repetitive and eminently forgettable "Untitled" to introduce these works, I've promoted their date-place citations to titles: "August, 1959—Albuquerque."

As Ed would likely say of this arrangement, "It ain't art, but it works."

Abbey's *Apples* also work. As the widely respected southwestern poet Leonard "Red" Bird (*River of Lost Souls*) commented after reading a draft of *Earth Apples* . . . "This collection carries Abbey's voice, his eye for significant detail, his humor, his lust for life and his anger at all who would destroy or succumb. In his poetry, as in his novels and essays, Abbey was a man of passions. He *felt* . . . love, loneliness, rage, regret, despair, joy and hope."

Just so.

Michael McCurdy is an American master of the woodcut and scratch-board arts, and Clarke Abbey and I are delighted to have his work illustrating and illuminating this little volume—as, I feel certain, would be Ed himself.

For their essential help in bringing this collection to print, I thank Clarke Cartwright Abbey (the best thing that ever happened to old Cactus Ed); Leonard "Red" Bird (teacher, adviser, poet, friend); James Hepworth, Larry Hartsfield, Richard Shelton, and the Durango Public Library research staff (lifesavers, one and all); Roger Myers, Peter Steere and their energetic crew at the University of Arizona's Special Collections Library; Bob Weil at St. Martin's Press; and (always) Caroline.

—DAVID PETERSEN
San Juan Mountains, Colorado
March 1994

CONFESSIONS

(1951–1965)

The Whole Fucking Crew

(November, 1951—Edinburgh, Scotland)

The Gods who once were pleased to stay
Somewhere in outer space
Have now, alas, come down to Earth
And run the God-damned place.
Just look around, they're everywhere,
They mean to freeze or fry us—
STALIN, TRUMAN, MacARTHUR, LUCE,
    CHURCHILL, TAFT, POPE PIUS.
They're getting bigger all the time,
No more a harmless myth—
EISENHOWER, ACHESON, VISHINSKY,
    SHERMAN SMITH.
And all their spies are hard at work
From Moscow to Vancouver—
L. BERIA, McCARRAN, JOE McCARTHY,
    G-MAN HOOVER.
In such a mess as this, what are
Honest men to do?—
Load up our guns, I say, and shoot
THE WHOLE FUCKING CREW.

November, 1951—Edinburgh

belted mountain!
gods' home!
heap rock heap!

[Editor's Note: This likely is a reference to King Arthur's Seat, a basaltic (volcanic) core that stands as an Edinburgh-area landmark.]

December, 1951—Edinburgh

Under blankets of European air,
Hovering in green fog and gray memory,
Sea-chills creeping over skin and hair,
And night-dream badly mixed with day-time
     memory;—
Cathedrals, squirming with detail, everywhere,
Humanity's bad dream paralyzed in rock,
And gargoyles leaking rusty tears, and bare
Screams scored in air, eyeballs braced for shock;
Large priests with briefcases on bicycles;
In an old woman's arms a starving brat,
The proud aristocrat of death; sickles
Crossing hammers in crayon red on flat
Yellow walls where buried bullets wait
For hate to resurrect them; such a freight
Of age, nations sinking under history,
Has a flattening effect, depresses
Minds and hearts amazingly, compresses
People into bundles without mystery.

[Editor's Note: Edinburgh's St. Giles Cathedral, considered by many as among the ugliest buildings in all of Britain and Europe, may likely have inspired this work.]

December, 1951—Edinburgh II

Land of the pilgrims' pride,
Land where my fathers died,
From every mountainside
LET FREEDOM RING:
While this America settles in the mold . . .
A wind is rising and the rivers flow.
Sail on, sail on!
O hand of fire, thou gatherest, thou gatherest!
With malice toward none—
All aboard for the Paradise Express!
Give me your huddled masses yearning—
Kiss of our agony!
Nothing to fear but FDR himself.
A voice comes to me in the night, saying—
Call me Ishmael.
Lost voices from the past, wind-borne, saying—
Get the hell out of that wagon!
O lost, and by the wind grieved, ghost come
    back again!

My name is Jonathan Troy.
I hear America singing. . . .

[Editor's Note: Jonathan Troy is the protagonist of Abbey's first and little known novel, *Jonathan Troy*.]

February, 1952—Edinburgh

The oboe: I sing to you of a love beyond all loves
a scene in complete silence;
motion without sound, as in a silent film
pure as a negative Wassermann.

Verse Provoked by a Recent Visit to the Stacks

All the forlorn futile faces
Drifting, ghostly, through the iron and book-filled
    cages
In a sunken filtered light remote from day—
How often in these melancholy places
(so like old dungeons in the Middle, Dark or Christian
    Ages)
Am I impelled by fearful piety to pray:
O Lord, preserve me from the fate of these poor hacks
Who bury their lives in library stacks.

January, 1952—Majorca

New music is a desert range
where arid canyons thread an unexpected maze.
There is nothing there, nothing there.
No cities, gods or dreams of men,
no further art, no hope, no despair.
Nothing but a nothingness that dumbs
the heart's sick wail, the mind's nervous drums.

January, 1952—Majorca II

This body of mine—
bawdy, vile, full of bones,
odd noises, smells, bass tones,
glands, organs, jelly-sacs,
vapors, rheums, humors, packs
of fat, oil and grease; a bag
of bubbles, tricks, with a flag
of hair on top, a crotch of hair
and dangling sex below where
the bag divides and stands upright.
Is this, Narcissus, my inheritance,
wobbling muscles on a stagger-stance,
and all the eyes' fond roving,
a lip to touch and nothing more,
the mouth of Heaven's whore?
Mother, Jesus, Mary, Earth, Jehoshaphat,
I want rather more than that!

March, 1952—Edinburgh

O love, let us be true to one another, while the gods fall and the skies split open in thunder. Let us be true to Art, the cause of beauty—dedicate our lives and all the rest. Let us be true to our own humanity, not forgetting others, that we who are more fortunate and beautiful than all the saints in a painted heaven ever can be—that we may be in motion, always growing, and but dream of death.

April, 1952—on the North Sea

In old England's iron cities stare
Too many burnt-out faces dead with care,
Too many blighted spirits on their knees,
Too many children starved for sky and trees.
Here's a labor for the young: Set right
The wrongs
Of centuries.

April, 1952—on the North Sea II

What is more beautiful than red streaming
Banners on the wind screaming
"Fire! Revenge! Death to Kings! Life
to the new world of the heart's dreaming!"?

Brief Speech to a Weather Vane

(April, 1952—on the North Sea)

One bird, metal-hearted, tin-feathered,
Turning with the wind—
Other, older birds than you have weathered
Nature's idiot bluster, tinned
Corrosion and her graveward shove.
Have survived, and even learned to love
What never loves, and to create
Music out of empty hate.

April, 1952—on the North Sea III

If nothing more, let this at least be said:
"He remembered, as he carved his steak,
the overworked and underfed."

May, 1952—Norway

The great were great; lived wondrous days . . .
Left names as strong as thunder,
Bright as lightning—but
They are dead—
And you and I are living.
The old names arch against the sky
And shine by the sun;
Immortal in memory, their owners never die,
Completely. But every one
Is gone in body now, dissolved in earth—
No eyes to see the red
Flamingo fly, no mouth to taste the worth
of heavy oranges, dead
And gone the nerves that knew
A girl's warm and curving breasts—
While you and I are true
To life and one another, all their glory rests
In death. Let them keep it. Do not fear,
It's *you* that *I* want. Now. Here.

May, 1952—Norway II

To those who call themselves "Communist,"
And their friends, such as they are, "Comrade,"
And have betrayed the youngest dream of man,
And have turned upon their own people,
And have insulted the hope of minds now dead,
And have mirrored in their work the shape of the
    Enemy;
To all of these—I offer
The cold knife of pity.

Feudalism

(December, 1954—Albuquerque ... "Duke City")

The Duke and his family,
Proud ancestral name of a thousand years,
And all around the earth they owned,
Worked by the squat brown peasantry
Who sprang, spontaneously generated,
Without pasts, from the soil itself.

[Editor's Note: The subject of this poem, no doubt, was the Duke of Alburquerque, Viceroy of New Spain, who in 1706 named the new pueblo after himself. The initial *r* was later dropped from the spelling.]

Terror and Desire

(June, 1956—Arches)

The light floods out and falls
for the last time today
over the canyon walls
where the tiger lizards play.
Where the scorpions play.

West, the nighthawks circle,
cry, plunge and kill,
in the sun's cool fire
flared above the hill.
Dying over the hill.

(While under the juniper tree,
with a cold elegance,
the rattlesnake glides,
death in his glance.
Hunger in his glance.)

The night creeps after the sun
with the faith of a lover,
or the stealth of one
with hate to uncover.
With fear to uncover.

I think that I could follow
and walk through fire,
forever, into that great hollow
of flame and desire.
Of terror and desire.

The Wild Dove

(June, 1956—Arches National Monument, Utah)

The wild dove calls at evening
From the canyon's lee,
Mourning, the soft notes falling,
Calling me.
Calling me, turning me
From my tales and fears
With the music of a sorrow
Beyond tears.
Beyond tears, beneath grief,
Beyond my human ken;
A song of the earth before,
And after, men.
And after men; as if
The defeat of love
Were a secret known only to me
And the wild dove.

(Rejected by *Atlantic, Chicago Review, Arizona Quarterly,
Southwestern Review, Grecourt Review*—E.A.)

Flash Flood

(July, 1956—Arches)

A flick of lightning to the north
where dun clouds grumble—
while here in the middle of the wash
black beetles tumble
and horned toads fumble
over sand as dry as bone
and hard-baked mud and glaring stone.

Nothing here suggests disaster
for the ants' shrewd play;
their busy commerce for tomorrow
shows no care for today;
but a mile away
and rolling closer in a scum of mud
comes the hissing lapping blind mouth of the flood.

Through the tamarisk whine the flies
in pure fat units of conceit
as if the sun and the afternoon

and blood and the smells and the heat
and something to eat
would be available forever, never die
beyond the fixed imagination of a fly.

The flood comes, crawls thickly by, roaring
with self-applause, a loud
spongy smothering liquid avalanche:
great ant-civilizations drown,
worlds go down,
trees go under, the mud bank breaks
and deep down underneath the bedrock shakes.

[Editor's Note: The above version appears as revised for *Desert Solitaire*.]

August, 1956—Arches

Once more before I fade and rot
Let love come
Come to me let it come
As the wren to the canyon
The berry to the juniper
The tassel to corn
O let love come and grow within me
Like an angel-child, like a child-angel,
Descending a moon-ray
Like a plume of tamarisk
Falling on grass.

August, 1956—Arches II

*(Cock-Brained Mary sings as she wallops the office
    floor with a foul and raggedy mop):*

Now, once more before I go
into the sterile afternoon,
let love come to me;
let love
let love come, come to me.
For I have need of thee,
child of earth, child of man,
as the hardening crust of the desert
has need of rain,
and the leaf of light,
as the drying juniper seed
abandoned on rock
has need of darkness and warmth.
Come then, once more,
sweet brave green silent
face of, form of—
oh sweet and silent
shape of love . . .
to me.

(And Blue-Balled Jim, clipping his toenails with a hatchet,
    sings this pretty tune):

Black sun
Black sun of my heart!
Blast down your killing
love, your dark fire,
carbon and cancer,
death-dance, desire.
Eat of my heart!
Eat, burn, kill, rape
and re-generate.
Endlessly wheeling, dancing,
draw life out of hate—
O day's eye! star's art!
O black black sun of my heart!

August, 1959—Albuquerque

Gawd bless Amelika
Land of the flea
Where the fat shits
And the big shits
On the multitudes pee.

The Writer

(June, 1963—Hoboken)

On a cold sea, empty of life,
Appeared
A solitary craft.

Ditty

(November, 1964—Hoboken)

(to be sung to the tune of "I Gave My Love A Cherry")

I gave my love a nickel,
A nickel and three dimes,
And sent her out to fetch me
The Sunday *N.Y. Times.*

But when she came back to me
Her love I did refuse,
Because what she had brought me was
The *N.Y. Daily News.*

July, 1965—Arches

A woman waits for me. (Ho!)
I am he who aches with amorous love.
And a quick connection for lunch. (*Chuff! Chuff!*)
Lewd old man + clean little girl = perfect couple.

Episodes and Visions

(circa 1956, from Desert Solitaire)

"Ranger, where is Arches National Monument?"
"I don't know, mister. But I can tell you where it was."

A Few Appropriate Lines from Burns

(circa 1956, from Desert Solitaire)

Green grow the rashes, O!
Green grow the rashes, O!
The lasses they have cozy bores,
The widows all have gashes, O!

A Maxim

(October, 1965—Home, Pennsylvania)

(for the hearth of brother Paul's new fireplace)

Gaze into the fire, remembering,
All is fire.—Heraclitus

Fire is life; life is a flame. Life is fire. Eternal fire.
Here burns a portion of the sun.
Who are we? Where do we come from? Where are we
    going?
Non omnis moriar.
In fire is truth. *In flammas veritas.*
I discovered in my heart, in the middle of winter,
an invisible summer.
Go thou my incense upward from this hearth,
And ask the gods to pardon one clear flame.

BOOK I

Poems for Judy

[Editor's Note: Judy Pepper was Abbey's third wife (of five) and the mother of his eldest daughter (of two), Susie. Judy died of leukemia in 1970, at the age of twenty-seven.]

Love Letter

The land is lovely here,
more beautiful every day.
The golden light of autumn now appears,
not in the sky but in the flowers—
matchweed, rabbitbrush, prince's plume,
beeplant, mule's-ears sunflower—
all blazing yellow.
A cold October wind blows from the mountains
although it's still September here below.
I must climb old Tukuhnikivats once more
before I leave.

The travelers are gone,
I roam the purple evenings alone,
thinking of you, treasuring
our trysting places, stopping each night
at that cove of sandstone
near the ancient juniper where we built a little fire
and last made love . . .
I kiss it where you lay.

The Gift

(May, 1963—Sunset Crater, Arizona)

There was a dry season in a dry country:
barren clouds above the mountain peaks,
blue delirium over the cliffs,
a hot wind moaning through the trees
of a dying forest. . . .

We waited, we all waited
for the soft and silver rain
to come and ease our thirst.
We waited, while our hearts
withered in the heat.

The first promise of a new season
came at evening in the form of evening light
(like the light in your eyes, your hair, your smile,
the soft glow on your arms).
The aspens shivered with hope.
The yellow pines stirred their heavy limbs.

The cliffrose opened its flowers
and a strange fierce joy sang through my heart,

in tune with the winds
and the ecstasy of the earth
and the singing of the wild and lonely sky.

Love Poem

(New Year's Day, 1964—Hoboken)

Under that leaking sky
the color of dead souls
where the snow is always gray
on asphalt and cement
and obscure birds
of dubious origin
seldom sing
or never sing at all
in the naked elms—
we found, somehow, you and I,
through the confusion
and brutal dullness
of the city falling in its sickness—
the shock of something wild
and secret, almost forgotten,
that flows through eyes
and nerves like fire—
yes, you and I,
in the good sweet luck
of our coming
together.

Song from the City

*(June, 1965—Room 12, Third Floor North, Klingenstein
Center, Mount Sinai Hospital, 99th and Madison, New
York City)*

There is a hermit thrush that sings
near a mountain spring,
its music like the flutesong
of some wild and lonely thing

under a silent sky. Far above
on the mountain's crest the snow
is melting now. The waters rush
down toward twilight, through the alpenglow

of evening. Smoke rises slowly
from an old campfire. A bird calls,
still, alone, in the clear dark.
And my heart falls.

Soaring Song

(October, 1967—San Francisco)

Yes—even after my death
you shall not escape me.
Reincarnate, I'll follow you
in the eyes of every hawk,
every falcon, vulture, eagle
that soars in whatever sky
you walk beneath,
all the earth over,
everywhere.

Yes—and when you die too,
and follow me into that deep
dark burning delirious blue
and become like me—
a kind of *bird*, a feathered thing—
why, then I'll seek you out
ten thousand feet above the sea;
and far beyond the world's rim
we'll meet and clasp and couple

close to the flaming sun
and scream the joy of our love
into the blaze of death
and burn like angels
down through the stars
past all the suns
to the world's beginning again.

North Rim

(July, 1970—Grand Canyon, Arizona)

Everything conspires to haunt me here
with memory and thought and sense of you:
the fragrant lupine and the quiet deer,
the hawk that soars against the icy blue
of noon, the silver aspen on whose bark
I carved your name and mine within a heart;
the night you came so softly in the dark;
the day I came to you at last—to part.

My darling girl, is there no end to love
which lives despite all loss, regret and tears?
that flourishes on mountain rock, above
the plain, and grows against the wind and years?
Let it be so. I'll consecrate my days
to loving love, and you, and all I praise.

Idle Music

Silver music in
an idle tune
dark laughter under
the haunted moon
—oh, the heart's brave
thunder dies so soon!

BOOK II

Occasions

A Simple-Minded Song of Hatred

(October, 1962—Hoboken)

Stated baldly—and why not?
I hate New York.
Why? Well—why not?
Why the hell not?
This vampire city, sucking the juice
from us poor country boys,
cracking hearts, smashing fingers
and toes, jabbing you in
the fucking eye, chewing the flesh
of a continent, breaking
our bones and lapping the marrow
up with a sibilant sucking sound
from a hundred million
dislocated joints, etc. etc.—
This wart, this chancre, this evil
carcinoma, feeding on the face
of a nation, befouling the earth
for a thousand miles. . . .
Your ship of asphalt, smoke and iron,

floating forever upriver into the heart,
obstructing the normal channels
of elimination, compounding
the national constipation, polygamous
city of— oh!—naked shame!
Island of madness! Death ship!
Concrescence of sickness, sore point,
needle of lunacy, scientistic
fantasy of electrical gardens,
impossible prison, lockstep bedlam,
oh towering carnival cell blocks
of schmuck-eating cannibals. . . .
Yes. Eight million pounds
of shit per day, record production,
setting new quotas, unlimited aspirations,
broken noses, split eyeballs and vaginal
fangs! City, I say, of horror!
City of nightmare! City of sorrow!
Madhouse! Shambles! Inferno!

Gather your strength, convoke your voltage
of light and glittering brains—
force it all through the unicorn tower—
burn a hole in the iron sky!

One Thing at a Time, for Christ's Sake

(October, 1962—Hoboken)

If we consider the sunflowers
in the railroad yards of Hoboken
we cannot, fairly, account for the grace
of the traffic converging in ranks
under armor and bellowing down
on the cops at the tunnel gates
and the music under the skirt
of a black-stockinged blonde walking home
from the factory doorway here.
So—? We take time out to approve
(if the barrage of noise will permit us
—that roar from the gun-barrel sky)
of the papers to be signed in quadruplicate,
the scream of the sirens, wine
on the rock of Weehawken, shipwreck and bricks,
sea-wrack and garbage cans,
TV dinners and indigestible love,
while steak floats on sweat and blood
where the brown boy slipped on the grease

on the road and the bus
(the driver makes change between fits
of scratching his scrotum)
crunches bumpily (brief scream)
over the body, rib cage and skull
smashed flat as a dog on the freeway,
and of course the crowd gathers
—why not?—to adore, drawn by the smell
of blood, and the money, where warriors grunt
like hogs hanging from hooks
in slaughterhouse chutes,
on a smoky day in July.

Manhattan at Twilight,
Seen from the Palisades

(June, 1965—Hoboken)

Who would believe the city could be so lovely?
The streets gashes of golden fire,
the towers glowing like blocks of radium,
filled with a rich, cool burning,
and the endless stream of the traffic
that flows by the glittering river
like a necklace strung with beads of light
and draped on the shoulders of the city;—
an island of electric magic to fill with awe
the mind and heart of some far voyager.

BOOK III

*Notes & Illuminations
from a Burning Book*

King Aethelstan to All Heads . . .

"Gif wiccan owwe wigleras mansworan, owwe morth-wyrhtan owwe fule afylede aebere horcwenan ahwahr on lande wurthan agytene, thonne fyrsie man of earde and claensie tha theode, owwe on earde forfare hi mid ealle, buton hi geswican and the deoper gebetan. . . ."

ABBEY'S TRANSLATION:
"If witches or weirds, man-swearers or murther-wroughters, or foul defiled open whore-queens, any-where in the land are gotten, then force them off earth, and cleanse the nation, or on earth forth fare them withal, until they beseech and deeply better get. . . ."

Pommes de Terre

The plow; the raw September earth; the massive-haunched and mighty-hoofed old bay clomping and farting down the furrow; Father holding the plow, my brother the reins, and me with a sack following, gathering the fruits of the overturned soil—the earth apples. . . .

Richly abundant, brown fat potatoes, thick as stars, appearing like miracles out of the barren, weedy, stony patch, thousands of big hefty solid spuds, bushel after bushel, a hundred bushels per acre, a mass of treasure from the earth. . . .

How our hands and eyes delighted in that harvest, how gladly we dragged our bulging gunnysacks to the wagon . . . a wagonful of potatoes! Dark, crusted with dirt, soil, earth, cool to the touch, good to eat even raw; we plowed the shabby-looking field and turned up nuggets, plenty, abundance, more than enough to last through the winter, more than we needed, riches unimagined. . . .

A Dream

The death of your father. Wild with vain regrets. Grasping your hand, clutching your warmth and pulse and blood and life. The darkness hanging round, specters in the corners of the room. The unimaginable annihilation—the nothing. The nothingness. Oh hang on, Paw, don't let go. Stay with us, old man, yet a little while longer. Fatal envy? I die, you live? All follow. We'll be with you soon. Blind man's bluff. Twilight time, hide and seek, *allee-allee-outs in free*. . . .

My thoughts gather like a dark cloud. Beware of lightning!

Last Rites

KY jelly
thymol iodide powder
5cc syringe
#19 or #20 hypodermoclysis needles (2)
#20 gauge 1mm needle (1)
70% rubbing alcohol
cotton balls
30cc Demerol @ 50mg per cc
Cocaine
    Codeine
        Demerol
            Seconal
                Morphine
                    Morphine
                      Morphine
                      Morphine
                        MORPHINE
                        MORPHINE

Peace & Plenty

10 gal crock of H_2O

1 can malt (w/hops)

5–10 lbs sugar or honey (honey's better)

1–5 cakes yeast

> Bottle at 2 degrees on Balling scale hydrometer
>
> Age two weeks
>
> (keep your phucking hands off them bottles!)
>
> Relax.
>
> Unlax.
>
> Exlax.
>
> A drink a day keeps the shrink away.

From a Sundown Legend

Weep, all you little rains;
wail, winds, wail. . . .

Where Is Your Rock?

... a juniper on a ledge of rock; overhead,
wild clouds in a violet sky; far below, the river;
and east, west, north, south—the distant
mountains.

Due Notice

Beware the weak, the timid, the small:
    they are dangerous.
Beware of love—more dangerous (and delicate)
    than dynamite.
Beware of thy wishes: they will come true.
Beware of your friends: your enemies you can trust.
Beware of the man who has no enemies.
Beware of wariness, which makes a coward
    of conscience.

What Zapata Said

The land,
like the sun,
like the air we breathe,
belongs to everyone—
and to no one.

Inconsolable Memories

—poverty, rural:

—chickens scratching in the dirt; green and white chickenshit on the kitchen doorstep; chained dogs howling under the front porch; creak of the porch swing at evening, as Sister entertains her beau; goddamned rooster crowing all day long, forlorn and horny as a unicorn; snot-nosed kids with shaven skulls (lice); the first muskrat in my trap-line, frozen in the ice; in search of the golden bee-tree; one dove calling from yonder hill. . . .

Essay on Time

Are there not
several modes of time?
    i.e. (1) (first, least and most trivial)
                 clock time, calendar time;
    then (2) solar time—day and night,
                 winter and summer;
    and (3) biological time—life-time,
                 time as measured by
                 the birth, growth, maturation,
                 reproduction, decay and death
                 of a living organism—
                 man, man-time, the human;
    and (4) the time of poetry, the time
                 of music, the time of love.

Past, present, future: mystery.
To live fully in the now—yes—
but not completely *now*, for if
we had no memory of what is past
and no awareness of the open future,

then our *present* would be meaningless—
we'd live like grubs in a rotten log,
with no more than the consciousness of worms.

And (5)   sidereal time—the life of stars.
           Sidereal . . .

And (6)   desert time: the stillnesses
           and music of sky and rock,
           the movement of wind on sand;
And (7)   river time. River time. The living flow.
           I am haunted by the sound of rivers' flow.
And (8)   the time of love—the birth
           and blossoming, the fruitfulness
           of love, the slow decline,
           the fading death of love,
           the end and emptiness.

Long Poem: A Few Words for Some of My Contemporaries

To Pablo Neruda
We'll never solve anything.
Granted.
But beware:
The vampire's shadow hangs above your country.
Come, let us sing together.

To John Chamberlain
Memo, John:
Instead of dragging the goddamned junkyard
into the art gallery
Why not heave the goddamned art gallery
into the junkyard?

To Judson Crews
Oh Laureate of Taos,
Of sagebrush and the human cunt,
Public Enemy Number One
Of all censors, postmasters and mystagogues—
I salute you. *Salve! Magister!*

TO ROBERT CREELEY
Your poems are short,
very short.
Mine
is bigger.

TO JOHN DEPUY
Madman and seer,
painter of the apocalyptic volcano of the world—
Companero, I am with you forever
in the glorious fraternity of the damned.

TO CARLOS FUENTES
The vultures gather
above the carcass of the dying bull.
The Revolution is dead.
Long live the Revolution.

TO J. EDGAR HOOVER
All good things must come to an end,
come to an end.

Go ahead, retire, don't be afraid, for godsake;
you'll get your pension,
we'll get you a job:
night watchman,
Tootsie Roll plant, Hoboken.

To B. Traven
Where is the true country of men?
Where are you, B. Traven?—
death-ship sailor,
treasure-seeker,
son of Macario, brother of the hanged—
where are you now?

To Ramon Sender
Young men in the slums
of Barcelona
speak of you, read you—
in seven red Sundays you'll re-conquer Spain.
Viva Bakunin!

To the Vietcong Soldier
Under the all-Amerikan
napalm boys,
whatever your name, whoever you are,
that Saigon embassy will once again be yours.
Remember Dien Bien Phu,
Remember Valley Forge. . . .

To Fidel
Goddamnit hombre, stop shooting people.
The real revolution begins
with the exile of the executioner.
Send your enemies
to the American Bay of Pigs—
Palm–Miami Beach—
they'll like it there.

To the Chase Manhattan Bank
Moloch still rises,
belching smog and garlic-flavored nerve gas,

towering above the city
like another Vampire State Building,
smile full of Cadillac crocodiles.

TO THE MAHARISHI WHAT'S-HIS-NAME
Oh hairy little man from what's-it-called,
from the sickliest nation on earth,
how grateful we are
to have you come
to teach us how to live.

[Editor's Note: Judson Crews was a friend from Abbey's 1950s Taos days;
Robert Creeley was a 1950s college friend from the University of New
Mexico; John DePuy— "Debris"—is a southwestern landscape painter
and one of Abbey's oldest and closest friends; B. Traven was the pen name
used by the mysterious author of *The Treasure of the Sierra Madre* and
other novels, and one of Abbey's literary influences.]

For the Old Man

(On His Seventy-Fifth Birthday)

Salud, mi padre, on this festive day!
Gawd bless yr whiskers & yr mortal clay.
(& while we're at it, bless old *Dios* too,
Who needs our blessings far more, Paw, than you
Need his—for is He not our creature?
Modeled on man in every manly feature?)
But now salute the man & not the Ghost,
Fuck the eternal, bless the mortal host
Of friends assembled at this sagging board
Of baked & basted fowl, of meat & pumpkin gourd.
(Don't frown at my clichés, there's more to come.)
Make water into wine, by Christ! the sum
Of all we know & can desire is seen
Within the distillated grape, serene,
To which yourself can testify, old horse
(Referring here to *our* old man, of course)
Who roars & rages in his grand old age
With all the beauty of a classic sage—
Oh one & noble, rare paternity,

High on 3/4 of a century!
Oh mountaineer of time, upon your dizzy height—
What lies beyond the day? beyond the night?
You need not answer, for we're climbing too
And soon enough will come to share the view
And share as well—why not?—that viney essence
Which does its best to justify our presence
Upon this bloody, sacrificial, beatific earth.
(Throw in an extra foot or two, who cares?
Does God not love to tangle pubic hairs?)
Which you, my woodsman Dad, have tramped
  since birth.
Salud! No man was ever more alive
Than *macho* our old man at seventy-five!

On the Birth of My Son

(After Su Tung-p'o)

Most fathers, when they have a son,
hope the boy will prove intelligent.
But I, through misapplied intelligence,
have wrecked my whole life,
and therefore hope my son
will grow up ignorant,
stupid and dull.
That way he'll lead a tranquil life
as a public administrator,
college president,
or United States Senator.

BOOK IV

Love's Bawdy

Frivolous Question

You say
you love me now.
Okay.
But will you love me
when I'm old
and bald and fat
and impotent
as an empty sock
and cold?

[Editor's Note: The first three poems in this section were read by poet-in-residence Edward Abbey to an overflowing—and audibly shocked—house at the University of Arizona in 1977.]

Two Profane Love Songs

1. no matter what you do baby
   no difference where you go
   I'll be watching you
   yes every time you see
   some big-assed bird in yr sky
   —hawk, eagle, buzzard, owl—
   why, that's me baby that's me
   re-in-carnate . . . re-meated . . .
   watching you fondly
   you sweet little fuck

2. don't cry sweetheart
   this was all foreseen
   and foreordained
   a fat million years ago . . .
   that you should come crying to my bed
   wearing my ragged pajamas
   that you should spread yr legs
   reluctant
   while I

explore your velvet pussy with my nose
slipping first my finger
and then my foot
into it
yes
all foretold
a million years ago.

I Wish

I wish my arms
were around you now
and your legs
around my neck
and my tongue
down in your throat
and your fingernails
in my kidneys
and my fingers
in your cheeks
and your hair
in my eyes and nose
and my ears
between your knees
and your nipples
on my belly
and my thing
inside your thing.
Okay. What else?
Oh yes—
and my feet
against the wall.

I Don't Want Them All

(I Just Want All the Ones I Want)

All the pretty girls—
Abbey's downfall, his destruction.
And his only regret—
the ones he missed. *Oh!*
The standing cock
hath no conscience. *Oh!*
How can I be true to one,
without being false to all the others?

Mornings in Santa Fe,
Dead in Death Valley

The tomatoes were still green
your coffee black and bitter,
but the taste of your sweet brown nipples
in my teeth reminded me
that I was home again.
Home at last, I thought, sliding in,
as if for once my weary drive
back and forth across this bloody continent
had come to a real garage.
Mirage. Within ten weeks
my idyll would be smashed
in the valley of rock and alkali,
horseshit and movie actors,
and all my pretty hopes banged out of shape again.

BOOK V

Desert Music

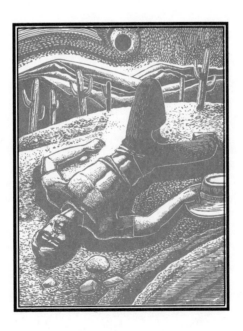

Black Sun

to lie alone in the desert
and stare at the sun
until the sun goes black. . . .

Black sun, black sun of my heart—
Strike down your shaking blaze of fire
Eat up my eyes and brain
Burn me clean and dry of all desire.

Black, black, sun in my heart—
Rain down your murderous love
Your flash and carbon, cancer and heat
Bake me sweet as a dove

Sweet as a stone, black as a bird
Flay me with fire to the bone
Wrap me and wash me in flame
And leave me clean and alone

On the lost shore of a river I know
In the strange-lit country of stone.

Down the River

(September, 1963—Sunset Crater, Arizona)

Let's go now, boys, down that river
where the blue herons stalk through the cane
and beaver swim against the current,
quiet, strong, steady as the river;
where the slick amber walls of sandstone
lean over the brown god's flow, rising up straight
into light and a thousand feet of vibrant space—

(withdraw)

That's for us: sandbars and reedy islands,
deep still canyons leading into peace,
glens with clear springs, the plume of tamarisk,
silence, clarity, the sharp prints of deer
on the shore, down from the mesas beyond.

Bring your girls, your bibles, your poems
and children, bring in your souls' and hearts' courage
to search and hope, and prepare, and wait,

while the world we knew drowns slowly
but with sure increasing certainty
into its predetermined swamp of madness.

(withdraw   withdraw)

Once there we will build on rock
a house of stone that will outlast
all of their wars and furies, their carnivals of despair,
keeping on the hearth a fire of juniper
and wild scrub oak to warm the hall
and praise your eyes, your speech, your hands,
saving some part of the old virtue

(withdraw   withdraw   withdraw)

until the smoke clears and the time comes
to leave the wilderness and build at last
on the poor black battered plains of man
that visionary city of the prophecies.

The Dry Season

All day long I watch the blue sublime sky
with its perfect clouds
and the rain that fades into nothing halfway down.
The wind blows, every day, all the time,
though not without variety: yesterday blowing hard,
today blowing harder.

My Chinese windbells tinkle
like spirits in bracelets all morning,
at noon, all afternoon and all through
the flat dead hours of the night.
We're not complaining, just stating the fact.
(Your lips are dry and cracked, sweetheart,
your eyes are red, and breathing's hard.)

Good God, we need some rain.

Perhaps I should light my signal fire
in the crater of the old volcano,
beat the drum, begin my little dance . . . ?

I don't know. It's the dry season,
the pine needles crackle under my boots
        like raw spaghetti,
dust rises at every step, the wind
        drives it into my face;
the fire danger is rated EXTREME.

The flowers wait, curled in their buds,
and even the cactus hesitates to bloom.

Rain! Christ, give us some rain.

All day long we stare at the beautiful sky
with its beautiful, perfect clouds. . . .

Ambition

(1965—Hoboken)

I wish to be
an inspector of volcanoes.
I want to study cloud formations
and memorize the wind
and learn by heart the habits of
the ponderosa pine.
While we sit here
in our air-conditioned offices
rattling fresh documents
and arranging new wars
wasting time and squandering eternity
some really great things
are happening OUT THERE.

> viz., a buzzard sails above Deadhorse Point
> five thousand feet above the Colorado River
> and rolling down the sands of Grand Gulch
> unseen by any human eye
> a rumbling flood pours down to meet

another at the mouth of Happy Jack Wash.
Magpies are wheeling through the blue
of Magpie Arch above the land of Moab
and way down far in Stillwater Canyon
a blue heron stalks beneath the plumes
of lavender tamarisk. My God
I'm missing it all
sitting here in this office
with the windows that don't open
sixty-seven floors above the street
reading the *New York Times*
world's funniest newspaper
(think of all those joyous young pines
with who-knows-what aspirations of their own
cut down to feed a pulp mill)
and staring through the glass
from time to time
down into the smoking lanes
of the world's busiest graveyard.

American Picnic

(November, 1967—Tucson)

(in a desert place)

There was a trace of rain last night:
but now the sun.
And the subtle nut-sweet odor
of creosote floats like smoke.
One lizard crawls with care
down the face of mica-glinting rock.
The sand, pink as coral, lies warm
beneath our bodies, firm and good
and yielding to our hands.
Our supper cooks upon the clear
slow passion of burning mesquite.
The autumn sun consoles
our naked limbs. Doves call
from the middle distance and a hawk
patrols the quiet, waiting, blue-gold hills.
Miles overhead, three gray shapes
pass silently, like sharks,
trailing vapor plumes across the tranquil sky.

(Rejected by *The Nation, Atlantic, Harper's.*—E.A.)

An Evening Star

Through the rosy desert glow
of the smoggy Phoenix twilight
—that air as soft and rich as honey—
we saw this girl come near:
"revoltingly young,"
"an ancient sixteen-year-old"
with the level gaze and steady eyes
and classical good looks
of a classical goddess
and we thought, my painter friend and I,
"There goes the night. We'll get no sleep
tonight. We're going to make fools
of ourselves tonight, thinking of this girl,
this oleander air, the sky,
that chromium planet on the west
signifying love, going down in the rose
of the sun . . ."

Desert Music

Midnight on the desert.
La Bohème on the radio.
Love in my thoughts, as always.
There has never been a day in my life
when I was not in love
with at least two, often three, four
or even more—women.
Judy and Susannah (bless them both)
sleeping in the next room.
Farewell to the desert for a while . . .
maybe return next year? Maybe.
Who knows.
Who cares?
Oh reveries of solitary
wandering. For all the crazy days
of my chaotic life—
perpetual improvisation
from month to month, year to year—
if I should live that long.
Sometimes I think I'll live to be

a wild old shaggy man of ninety-odd—
a shy shaman, wooly wizard witch doctor—
and then I think
I'll cash in my chips tomorrow,
in some way fashionably absurd:
motorcycle knotted 'round a power pole—
heart colliding with a poacher's bullet—
a high exhilarating fall from rotten rock
upon my sun-bedazzled head—
a mysterious disease from inner space—
or simply disappear. Disappear,
from everyone, myself included,
down in the grandest canyons of the soul.
Is suicide the only sensible solution?
Oh the charming fantasies
of one's own death,
more fun than comic books.
But I shall live a little longer.
The sleeping sounds of wife and child
are warrant enough for that.

Outside in the cactus fields
I hear the rodents scurry,
and farther off, under the moon,
the call of a great horned owl.
Buen cazador, mi compadre.

A Sonnet for Everett Ruess

(1983—Oracle, Arizona)

You walked into the radiance of death
through passageways of stillness, stone and light,
gold coin of cottonwoods, the spangled shade,
cascading song of canyon wren, the flight
of scarlet dragonflies at pools, the stain
of water on a curve of sand, the art
of roots that crack the monolith of time.

You know the crazy lust to probe the heart
of that which has no heart we could know,
toward the source, deep in the core, the maze,
the secret center where no bounds hold.

Hunter, brother, companion of our days:
that blessing you hunted, hunted too;
what you were seeking, is what found you.

CONFESSIONS

(1972–1989)

Last Thoughts While
Lost Below Lizard Rock

(July 26, 1972—Aravaipa Canyon, Arizona)

There was so much I wanted to say
    and did not say.
There was so much I wanted to do
    and did not do.
There was so much I wanted to be
    and never was.

Three Limericks

(August, 1977—Aztec Peak Lookout, Arizona)

#1

A modest young fellow named Morgan
Had a hideous sexual organ;
It resembled a log
Dredged up from a bog,
With a head on it just like a Gorgon.

#2

An old aging roué known as Drew
Looks back on his youth in sweet rue;
In the years of his might
He could do through the night
What it now takes him all night to do.

#3

An LDS bishop named Bundy
Used to wed a new wife every Sunday.
But his multiple matehood
Was ended by statehood:
Sic transit gloria mundi!

For Marcel Proust, et al.

(October, 1978—Aztec Peak Lookout, Arizona)

They praise the firm restraint with which you write;
I'm with them there, of course.
You use the bridle and the bit all right—
But where's the fucking horse?

For Clarke

(October, 1982—Tucson)

High in the redrock canyon land
We come for our honeymoon;
Married in bliss near the end of May
Would it last till the end of June?
You're selfish, she says, and mean and crass,
And dirty and ugly and old.
Quite true, I admit, but you have a sweet. . . !
If I may be so bold.
So we love one day and we battle the next,
And the music goes round and round;
We're on top of the mountain on Thursday eve
And by Friday we're underground.
Rising on wings of delight to fly
Just as high as lovebirds can sail;
Then sinking, barge-like, to the floor of the sea,
Low down as the shit of a whale.
But we'll struggle on through and outlive our tears,
Whether marriage be joy or a joke;
I don't give a damn if it takes forty years,
I'm cleaving to Clarke till I croak.

The Kowboy and His Kow

(March, 1989—Tucson)

Oh give me a home where the buffalo roam
Where the deer and the antelope play,
Where seldom is heard a bawling beef herd
And the flies are not swarming all day.

Yes, give me a home where the grizzer bears roam
Where the bighorn and wapiti play,
Where *never* is seen a hamburger machine
And the cowshit's not stinking all day.

*(I should recite this at the annual Cowboy Poet's
    Roundup.)*

[Editor's Note: This poem is the last entry that appeared in Abbey's jour-
nals before his death on March 14, 1989.]

Benedictio

Benedictio: May your trails be crooked, winding, lonesome, dangerous, leading to the most amazing views. May your mountains rise into and above the clouds. May your rivers flow without end, meandering through pastoral valleys tinkling with bells, past temples and castles and poets' towers into a dark primeval forest where tigers belch and monkeys howl, through miasmal and mysterious swamps and down into a desert of red rock, blue mesas, domes and pinnacles and grottoes of endless stone, and down again into a deep vast ancient unknown chasm where bars of sunlight blaze on profiled cliffs, where deer walk across the white sand beaches, where storms come and go as lightning clangs upon the high crags, where something strange and more beautiful and more full of wonder than your deepest dreams waits for you—beyond that next turning of the canyon walls.

So long.

About the Author

Edward Paul Abbey was born on January 29, 1927, on a hillside farm in rural Pennsylvania. He died on March 14, 1989, at his Tucson home. In his sixty-two years, Abbey published eight novels—including the comedic-eco-anarchistic *Monkey Wrench Gang*—and fourteen volumes of nonfiction, among them the American classic *Desert Solitaire*. Two of Abbey's novels have found their way to film, and a third is in the works. No other contemporary American literary and cultural figure is so widely loved, and hated, as Edward Abbey. "I write," he liked to say, "to entertain my friends and infuriate our enemies." He did both.

About the Editor

David Petersen knew Edward Abbey as a friend, a mentor, and a colleague in letters. In addition to this volume, Petersen also edited and introduced *Confessions of a Barbarian: Selections from the Journals of Edward Abbey*. Petersen was born in 1946 and lives today with his wife Caroline in a self-built cabin in the San Juan Mountains of southwestern Colorado. He is the author of three books of natural history, and has edited and introduced *Big Sky, Fair Land*, essays by Pulitzer-winning novelist A. B. Guthrie, Jr. Petersen's own essays have been included in several anthologies. He is currently writing a book about grizzly bears in Colorado.